ARTS & CRAFTS PRIMARY 1

Jane Martin

Art consultant:
Lissete Madrazo

Course consultant:
Harriet Thompson

BY ME

My name is:

....

....

....

Contents

Extra Art sections

0 Art is everywhere

1 What inspires artists?

2 Match.

1

2

3

4

a

b

c

d

What inspires you?

3 Look and circle.

a

animals

b

plants

c

food

d

people

e

landscapes

f

buildings

4 Draw and colour.

1 Lines and shapes

Swinging, Wassily Kandinsky. 1925

1 Read and trace.

Artists use different lines.

straight curved wavy zigzag

Artists use different shapes.

circle square triangle rectangle

We see lines and shapes at school.

2 What lines and shapes can you see in this painting?

2 Activity 1 3 Activity 2

3 Trace the lines and shapes.

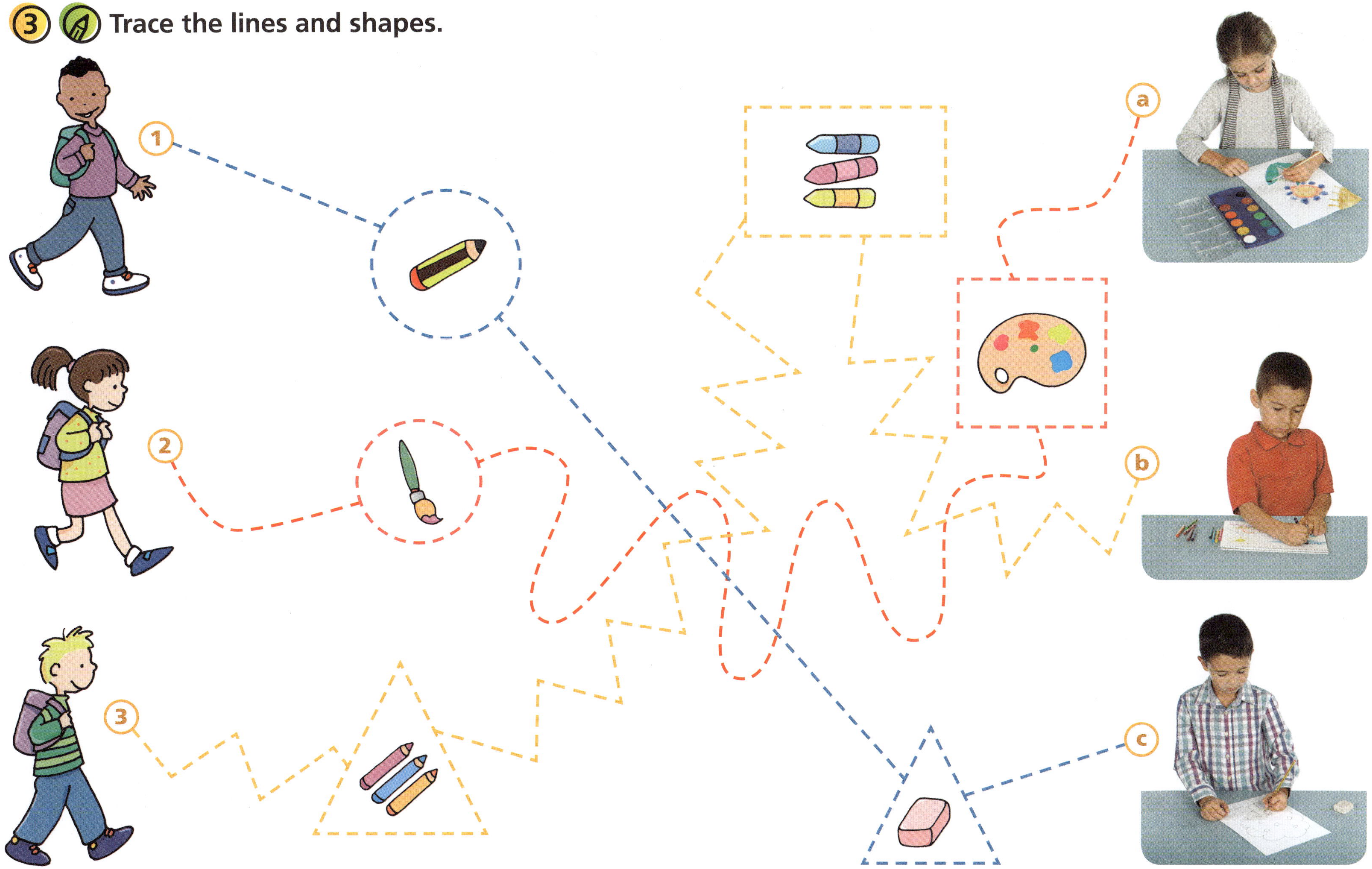

I feel happy at school.

1 Finish the teacher.

2 Draw a picture of you.

I can make a school with lines and shapes.

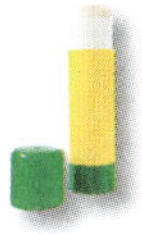

Step 1

Colour.

Step 2

Make a school.

Step 3

Glue.

Template page 65

2 Patterns

Comedians in the dressing room, Rafael Zabaleta. 1942

1 Read, trace and colour.

Artists use lines,

shapes,

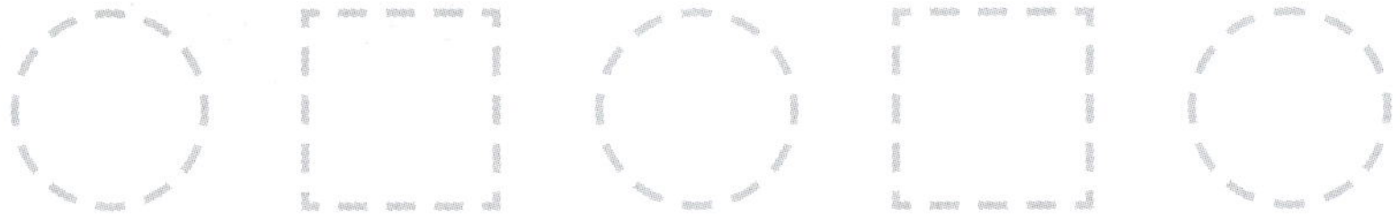

and colours

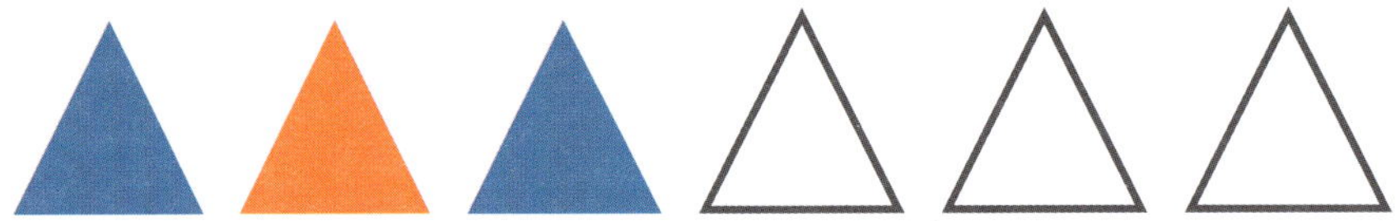

to make a pattern.

2 What lines, shapes and colours can you see in this painting?

4 Activity 1 5 Activity 2

3 Finish the patterns.

4 Make a pattern.

5 Finish the patterns. Colour.

I can see patterns

I can see patterns with my eyes.

1 Look at the numbers. Colour.

Colour by numbers

1 yellow
2 red
3 blue
4 orange
5 purple
6 green

2 Colour the pattern.

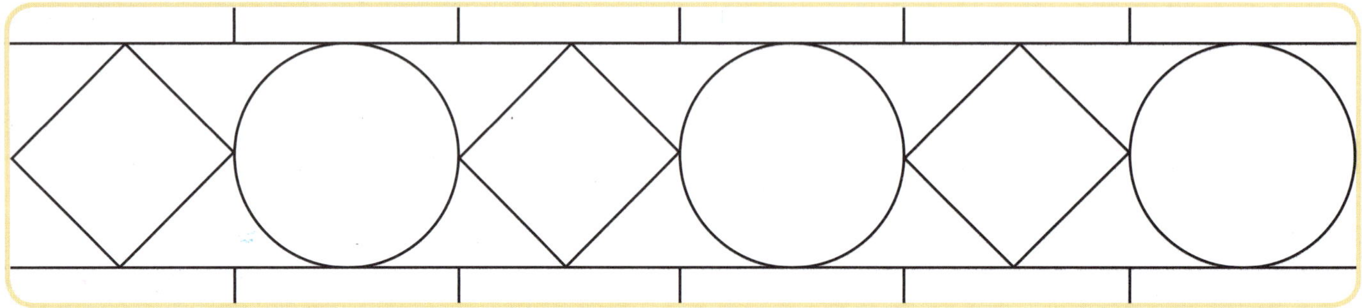

Patterns and music

I can hear patterns with my *ears*. There are patterns in music, too.

Step 1

Put the lentils in one bottle.

Step 2

Tape the two bottles.

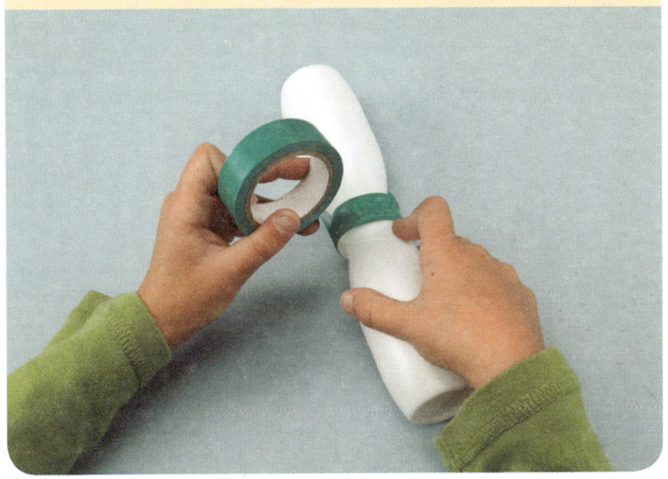

Step 3

Make a pattern.

3 Lines and colours

Zitronen, Paul Klee. 1939

1 Read and colour.

Artists use lines, shapes and colours to make Art.

Artists mix primary colours

blue red yellow

to make secondary colours.

green orange purple

2 What colours can you see in this painting?

6 Activity 1 7 Activity 2

green orange purple

3 Mix the primary colours. Write.

yellow + red =

yellow + blue =

red + blue =

We can move

I can move.
I can run, jump and dance.

1 Look, trace and draw.

I can run.

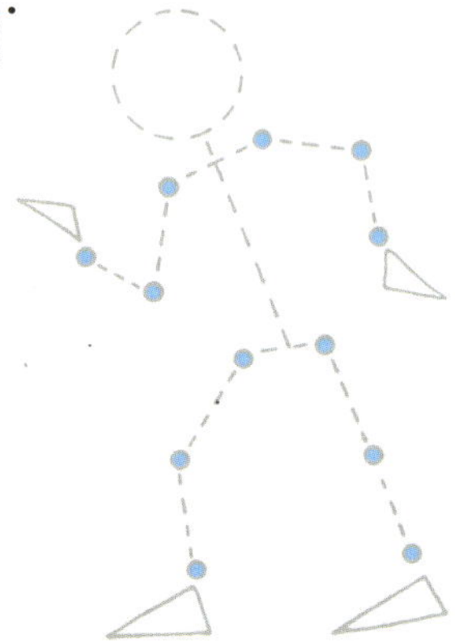

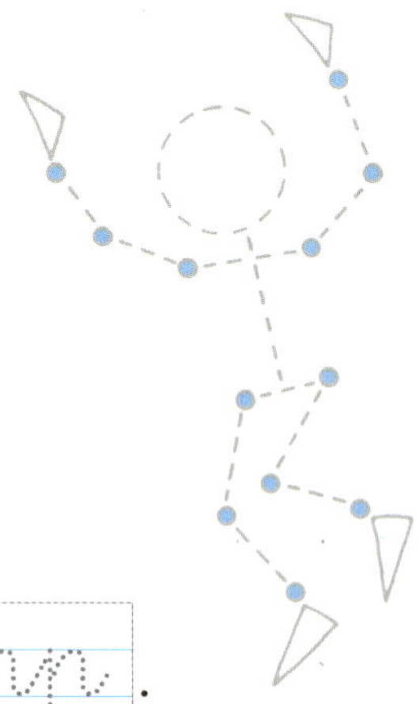

I can jump.

I can dance.

My body

I have got two **eyes**, two **ears**,
two **arms**, two **hands**,
two **legs** and two **feet**.

Step 1

Fold the paper. Draw one side of your body.

Step 2

Draw and colour lines and shapes.

Step 3

Fold and rub.

Step 4

Open.

REVIEW 1 Art in my home

Interior with Restful Paintings, Roy Lichtenstein. 1991

1 **Read and circle.**

This room has got lines, shapes and colours.

What colours can you see?

light colours

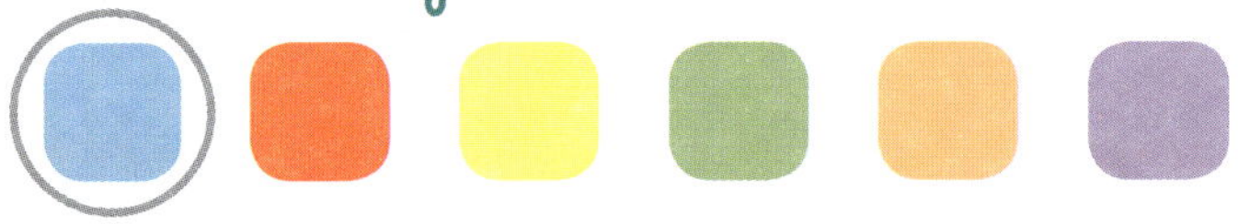

dark colours

2 What objects can you see in this painting?

8 Activity 1 9 Activity 2

Make patterns

We can see **patterns** in a room.

Step 1

Draw
a pattern.

Step 2

Colour
the pattern.

Step 3

Cut.

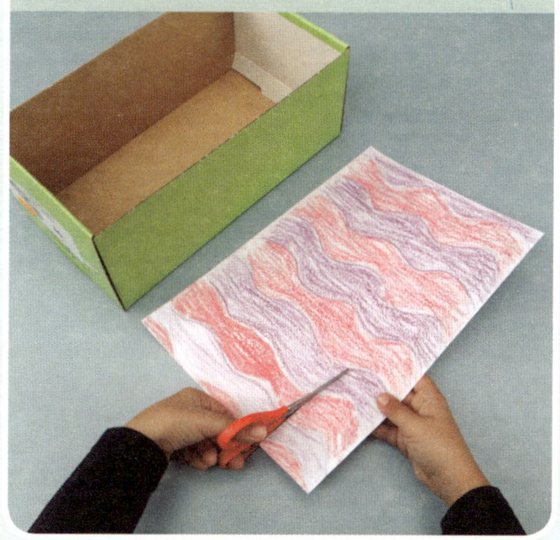

Step 4

Glue.

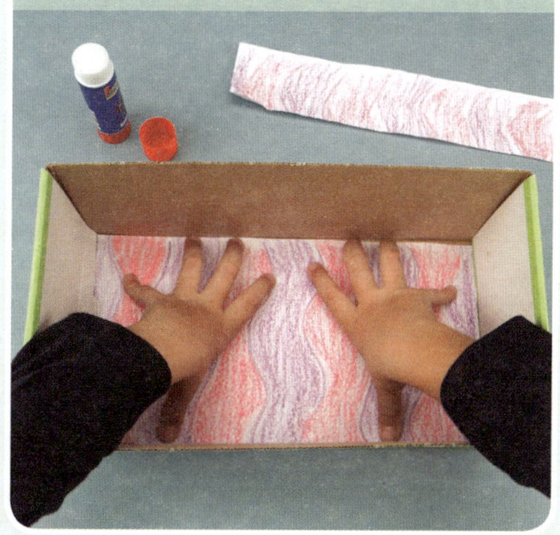

Rooms in my house

In a house, there are different rooms. There is a **living room**, a **kitchen**, a **bedroom** and a **bathroom**.

Next step:
Finish your house.

Step 5

Make furniture with plasticine.

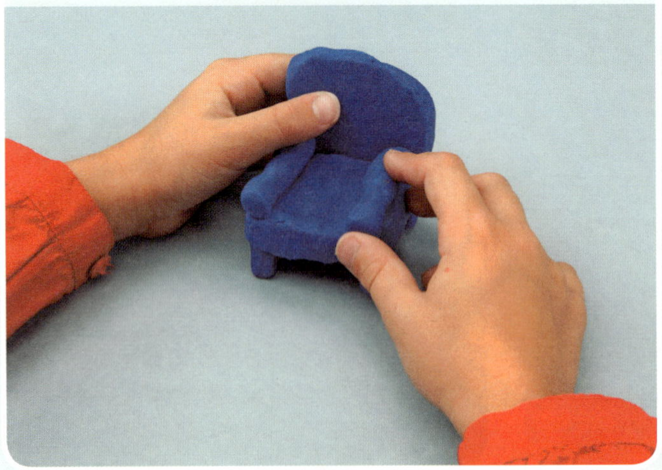

Step 6

Colour, cut and glue windows and doors.

Step 7

Put the objects in your room.

My house

Look at your artwork.

1 Circle.

In my *living room*, there is a...

In my *kitchen*, there is a...

In my *bedroom*, there is a...

In my *bathroom*, there is a...

2 Trace.

I can see lines and shapes.

3 Circle.

I can see light and dark colours.

Talk about your artwork.

4 Texture

Vertumnus, Giuseppe Arcimboldo. 1573

1 Read and trace.

A **portrait** is a picture of a person.

This portrait is made up of fruit and vegetables.

Fruit and vegetables have got different **textures**.

hard soft rough smooth

2 What fruit and vegetables can you see in this portrait?

11 Activity 1 12 Activity 2

3 Finish the textures. Write.

rough soft smooth

I can touch textures

I can **touch** textures.
I can **see** textures, too.

1 Cut out pictures of fruit and vegetables. Glue.

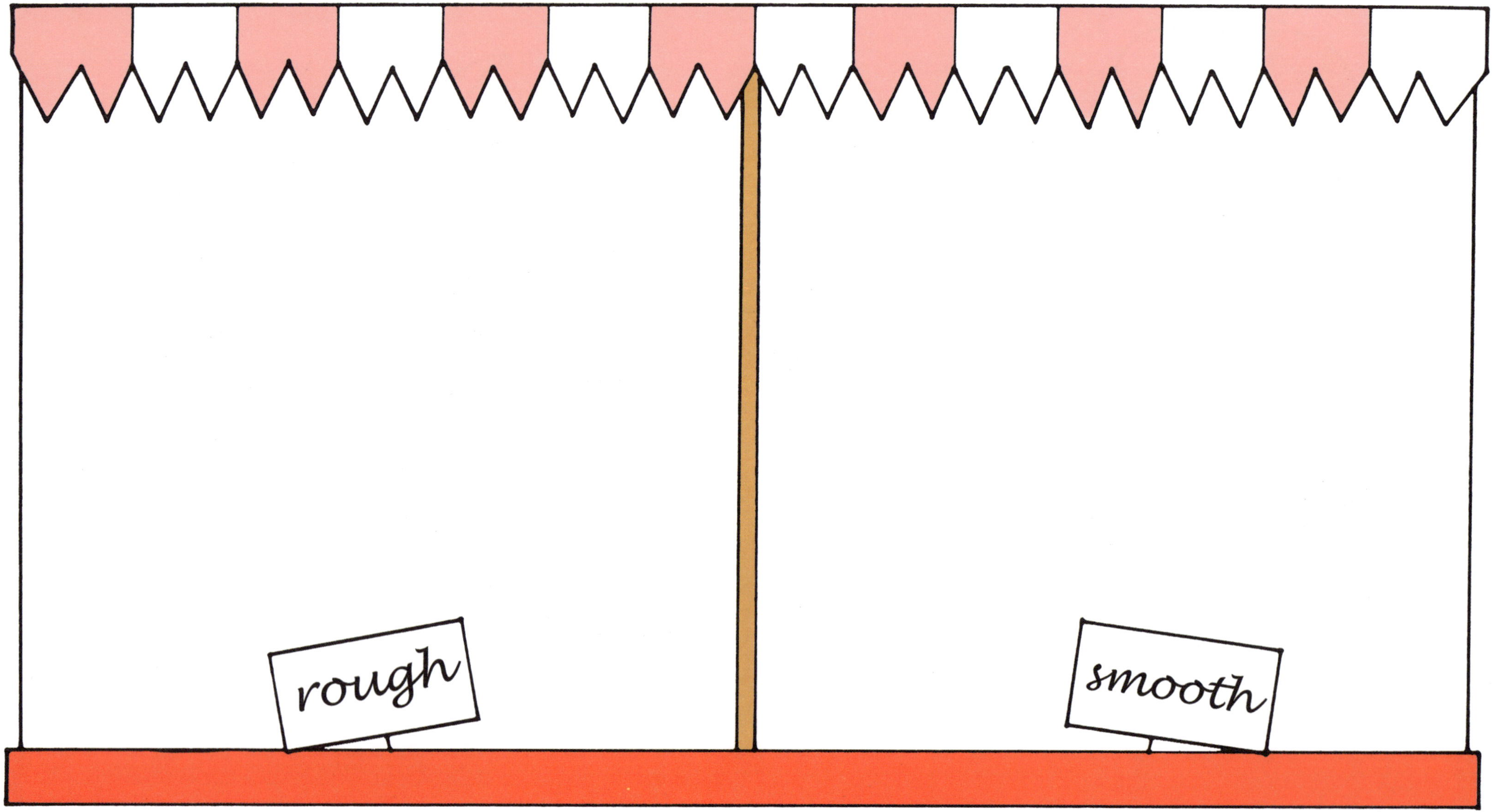

My portrait

I can make a portrait with fruit and vegetables.

Step 1

Draw and colour a fruit.

Step 2

Colour the fruit and vegetables.

Step 3

Make a face.

Step 4

Glue.

Template pages 67 and 69

5 Forms

Cat, Fernando Botero. 1987

1 Read and trace.

This is a sculpture of an animal.
It's made up of different forms.
Forms have got three dimensions.

Forms are 3-D.

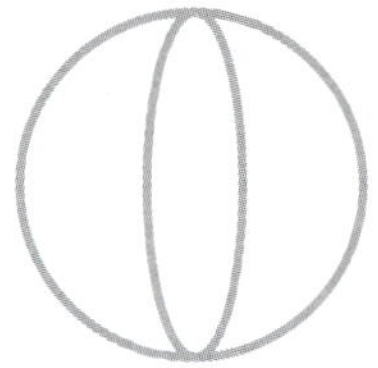
sphere

pyramid

cube

cylinder

2 What forms can you see in this sculpture?

13 Activity 1 14 Activity 2

3 Match.

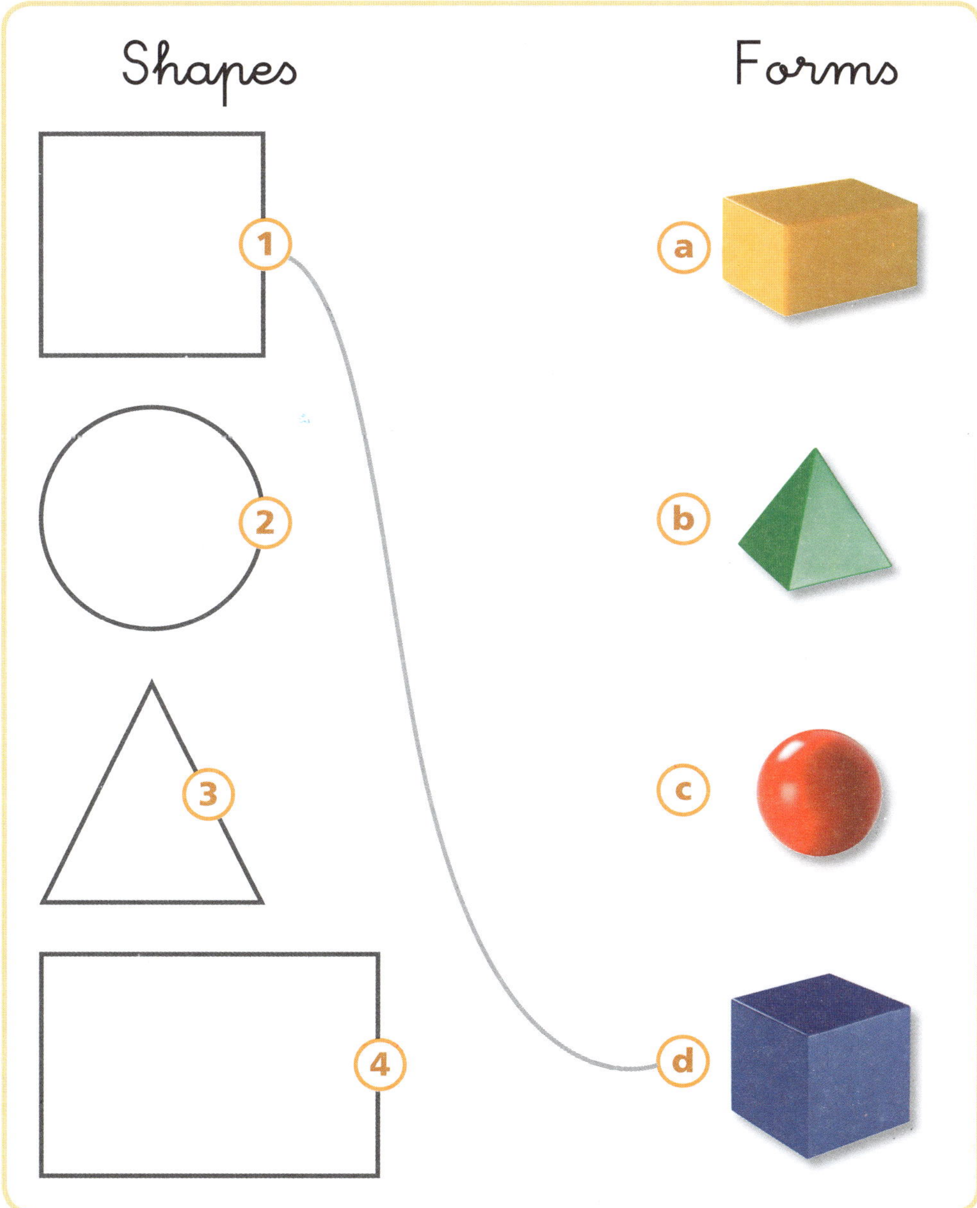

4 Trace the forms and draw a picture. Colour.

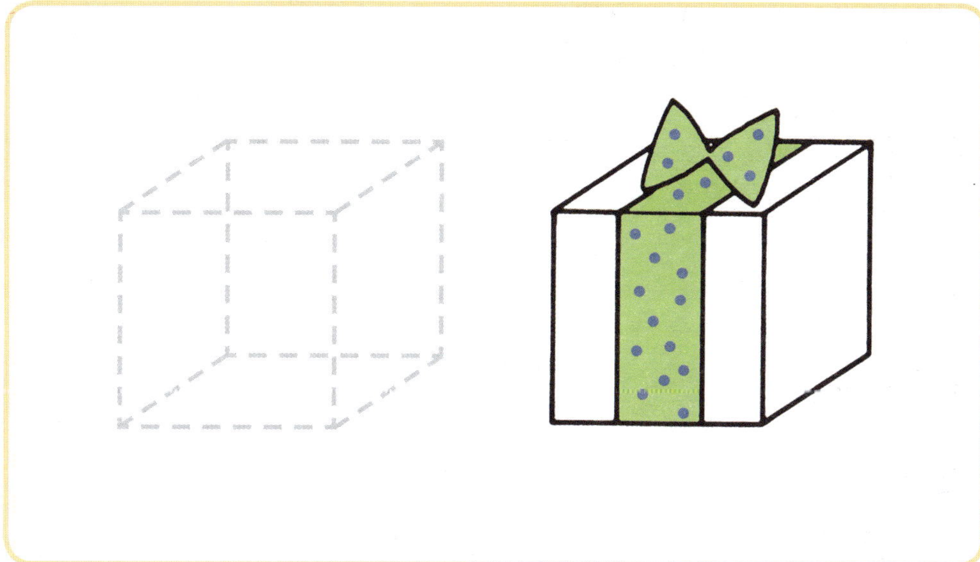

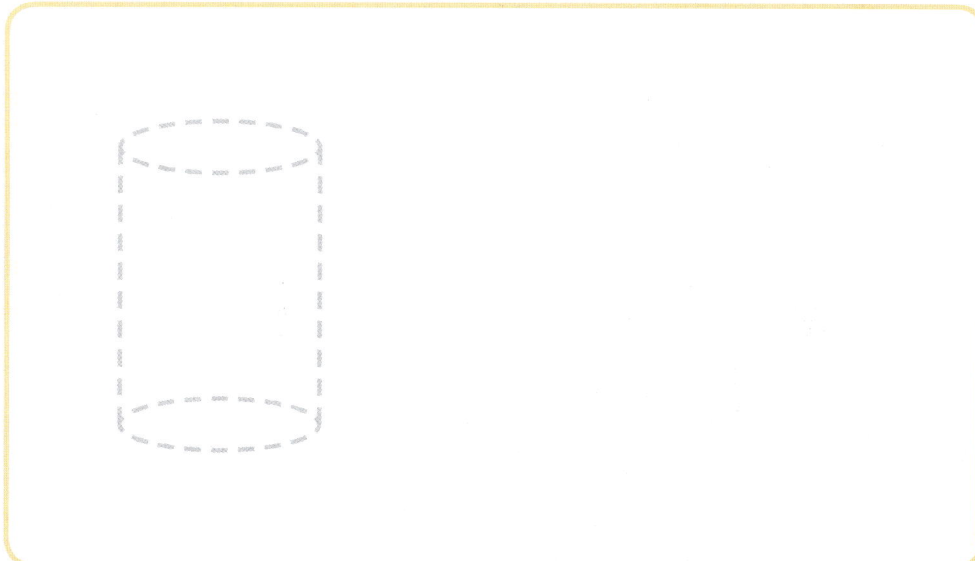

Animal forms

I can make an animal with shapes and forms.

1. Draw an animal with shapes.

2. Make your animal with forms.

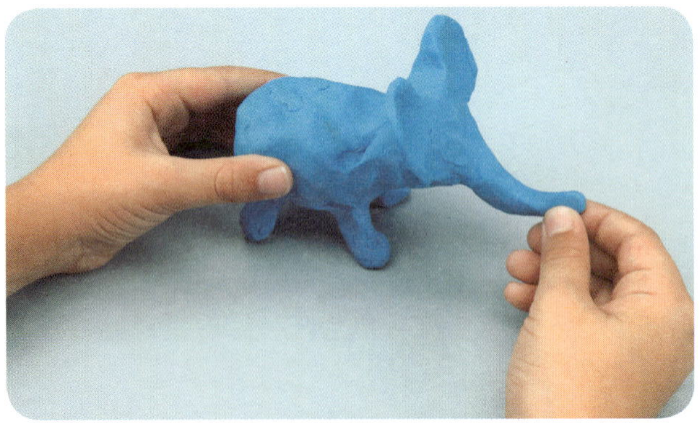

How many legs has your animal got? ______

Animal masks

I can use forms to make an animal mask.

Step 1

Colour and cut out the mask.

Step 2

Fold and glue.

Step 3

Decorate your mask.

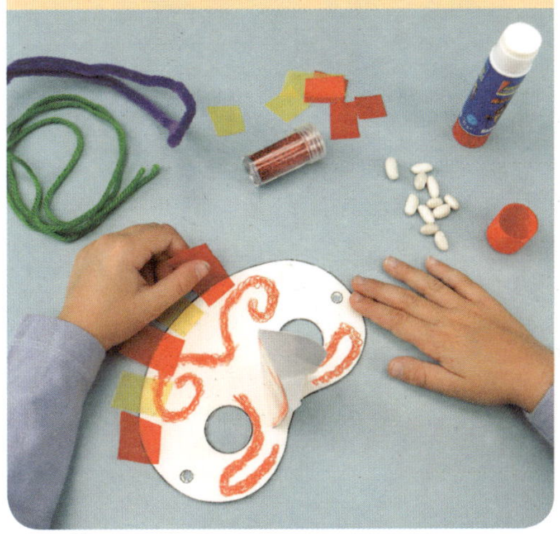

Step 4

Tie with cord and put it on.

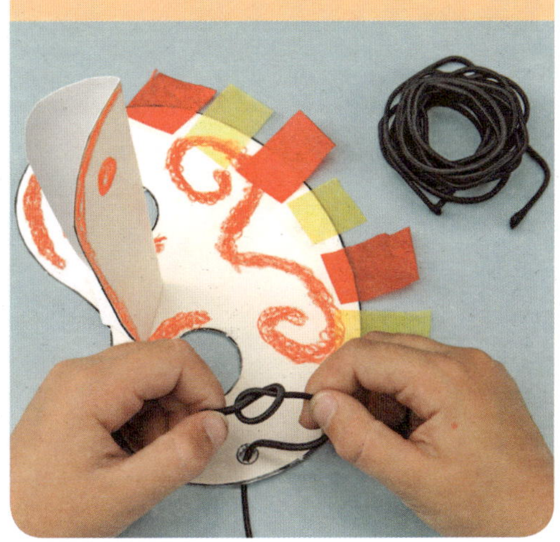

Template page 71

6 More shapes

Dome Garden, Juan Romero. 2004

1 Read and trace.

Artists use geometric shapes

and natural shapes.

We can see natural shapes in a garden.

2 What types of plants can you see in this painting?

15 Activity 1 16 Activity 2

3 Colour the geometric shapes blue and the natural shapes green.

I can see a .

My garden

I can make a garden with different shapes.

1 Draw geometric and natural shapes.

2 Colour the garden.

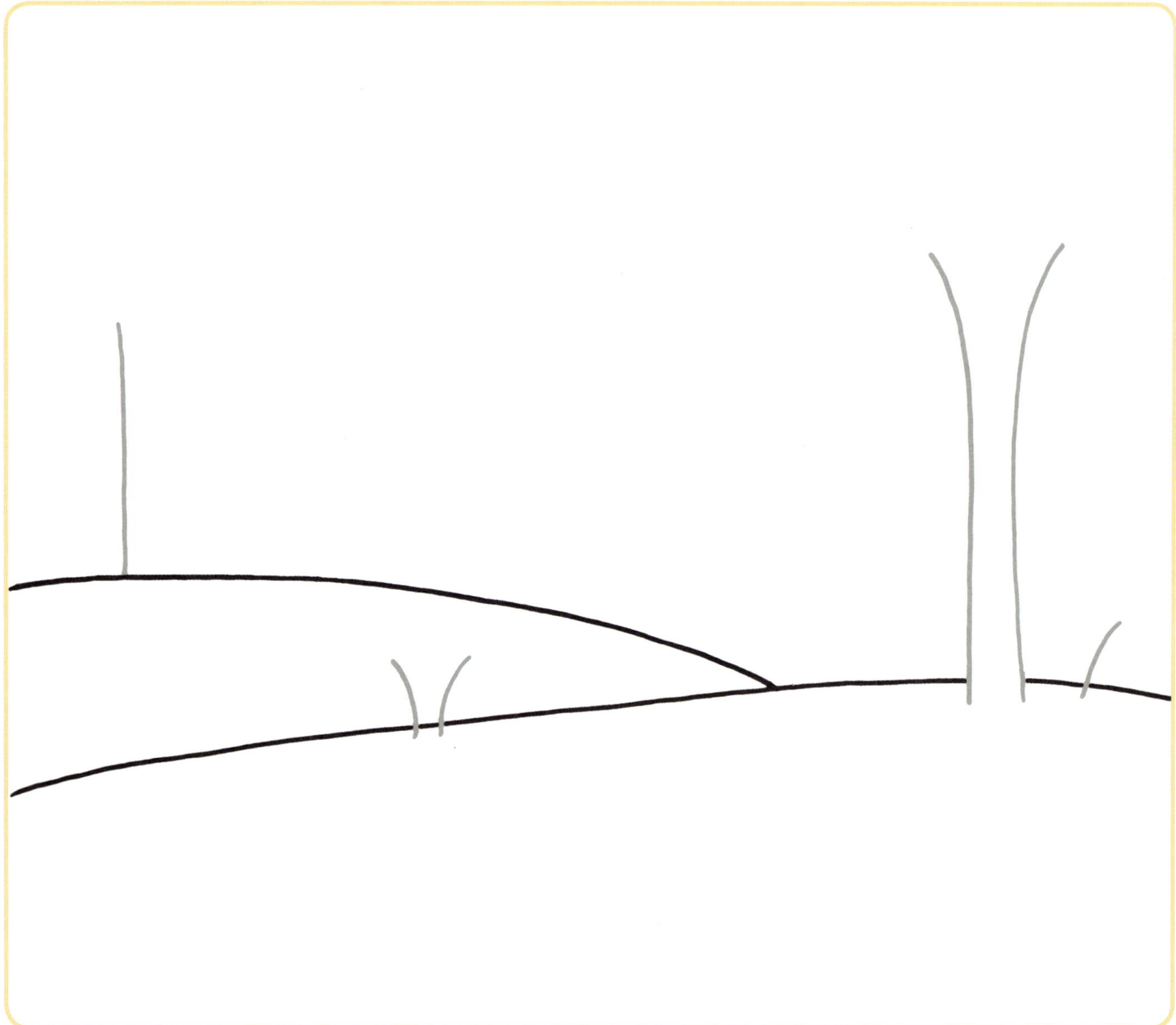

My garden grows

My garden grows. It grows up, down and all around.

Step 1

Fold, roll and twist the green paper.

Step 2

Fold, roll and twist the coloured paper.

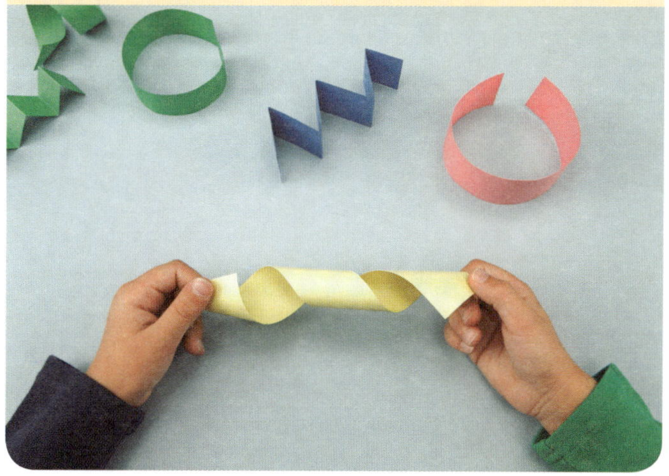

Step 3

Glue.

REVIEW 2 Art in my world

Composition 14, Sonia Delaunay. 1930

1 Read and circle.

Artists can fill space with lines, shapes, colours, textures and forms.

How does this artist fill space?

2 What can you see in this painting?

18 Activity 1 19 Activity 2

Draw water and air

Water and air move up, down and all around.

Step 1

Draw water with wavy lines and curved lines.

Step 2

Draw air with swirls and spirals.

Step 3

Paint.

My boat

A boat can float on water.
Air moves the boat.

Next step:
Make a boat race.

Step 4

Draw a sail
and patterns. Cut out.

Step 5

Make a boat
and draw texture.

Step 6

Glue the boat
and sail on the water.

A boat race

Look at your artwork.

1 Trace.

The water has got...

The air has got...

2 Draw and colour.

I can see patterns with lines, shapes and colours.

3 Draw and colour.

I can see rough and smooth textures.

rough

smooth

Talk about your artwork.

7 Buildings

① Read and write *same* or *different*.

There are different buildings
in a neighbourhood.

Some buildings are the same on both sides.

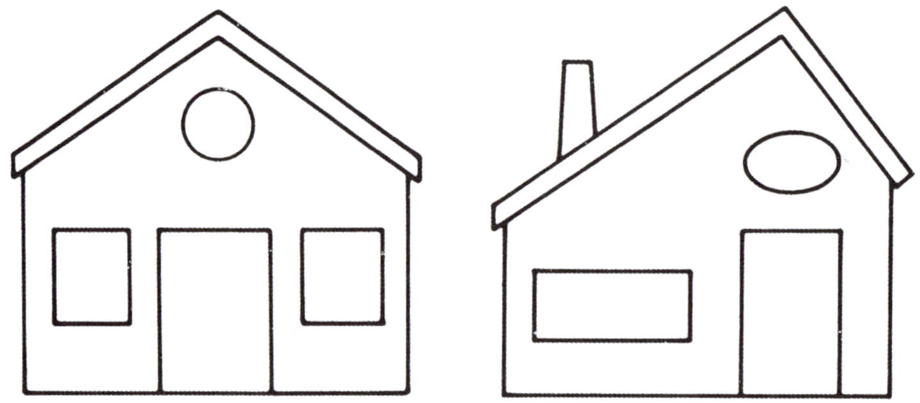

② Which building is the same on both sides?

20 Activity 1 21 Activity 2

3 Colour the windows and doors of this house. Same shape: red. Different shape: blue.

Finished? Draw a house that is the same on both sides.

In the neighbourhood

I can see different places in my neighbourhood.

1 Connect the dots. Complete the sign.

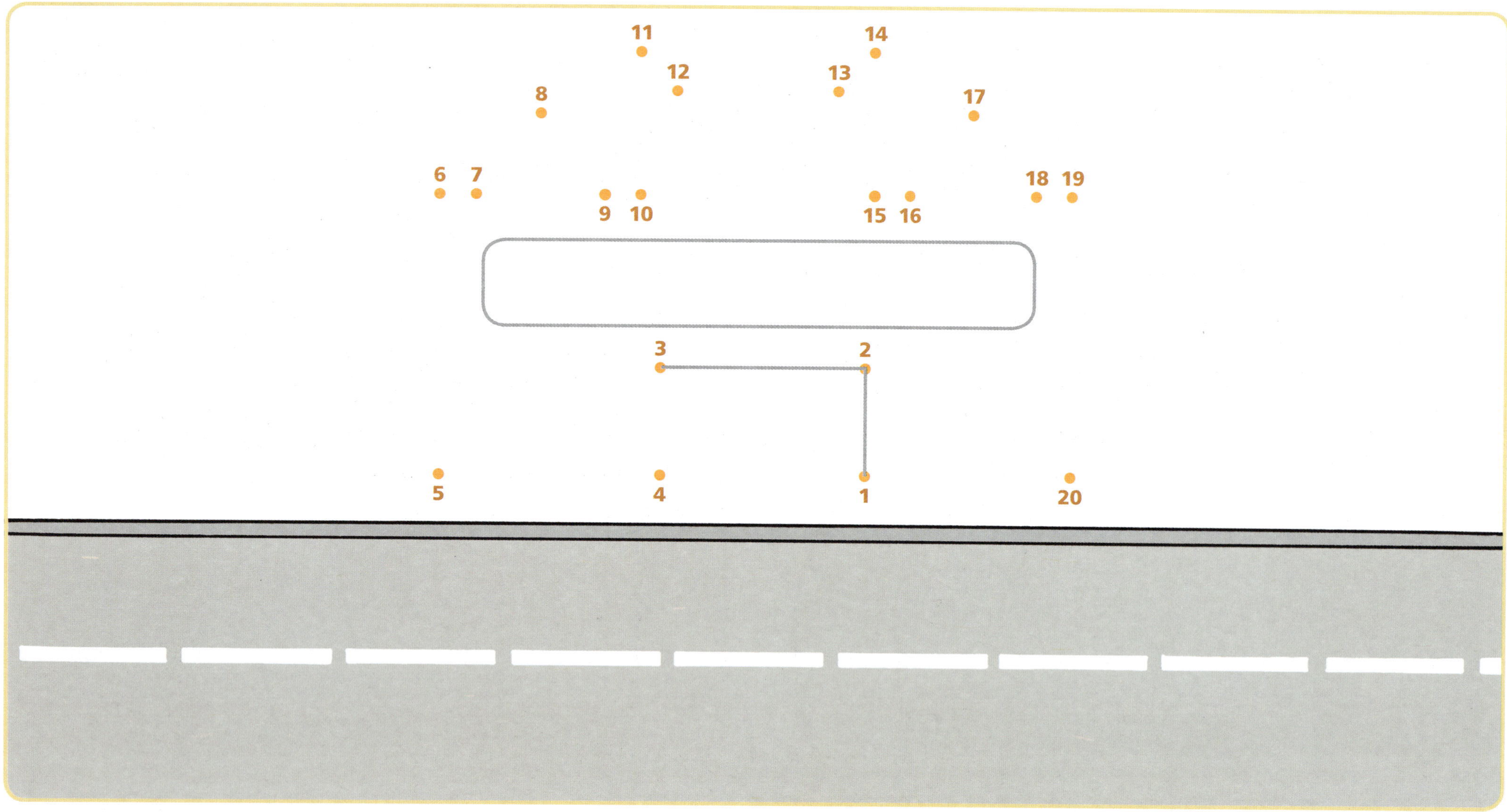

Finished? Draw and colour what's in your neighbourhood.

My neighbourhood

I can make a building that is the same on both sides.

Step 1

Fold and draw half a building.

Step 2

Cut out.

Step 3

Colour.

Step 4

Make a neighbourhood.

Finished? Add people, signs and forms of transport.

8 Landscapes

Mount Fuji, Utagawa Hiroshige. 1858

1 Read and point.

This is a landscape.

A landscape is an artwork of an outside scene.

There is a mountain at the back.

There is a lake in the middle.

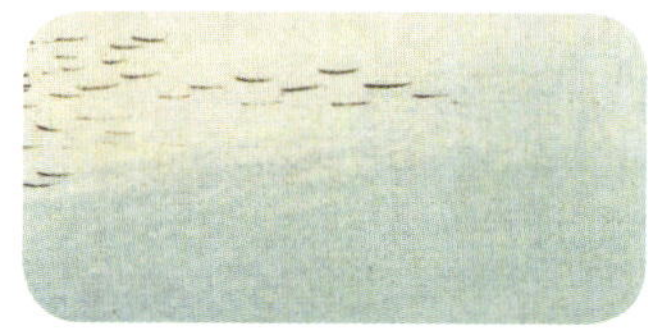

There are people at the front.

2 What can you see in this landscape?

22 Activity 1 23 Activity 2

3 Listen and draw.

Finished?
Add more objects.

24 Activity 3

Print a landscape

I can print a landscape with stamps.

1. **Make plasticine stamps and dip in paint.**

2. **Print mountains at the back, trees in the middle and a river at the front.**

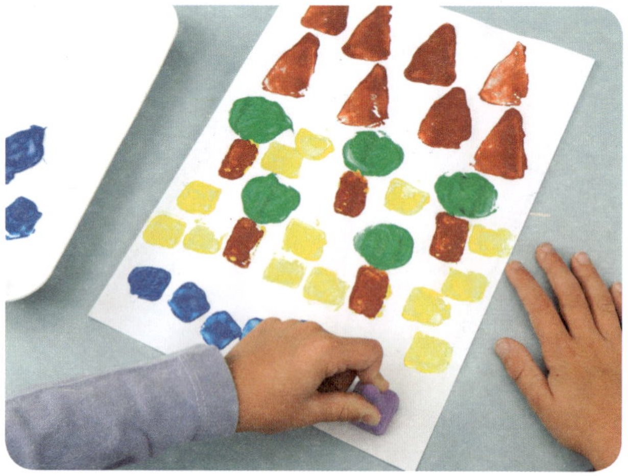

Finished? Wash the plasticine and make a model of your landscape.

Paper landscape

I can tear paper to make a landscape.

Step 1

Tear the coloured paper.

Step 2

Glue the sky and the Sun at the back.

Step 3

Glue the mountains in the middle.

Step 4

Glue the water at the front.

Finished? Print shapes.

9 More colours

Mosaic Sun, Antoni Gaudí. 1900-1914

1 Read and colour.

This is a mosaic Sun. Artists make mosaics with small coloured pieces.

Artists use warm colours

and cool colours.

2 Which warm colours and cool colours can you see in this mosaic?

25 Activity 1 26 Activity 2

3 Colour with warm colours.

4 Colour with cool colours.

Finished? Draw warm colour objects and cool colour objects.

Sun patterns

I can make patterns with warm and cool colours.

1. Continue the patterns.

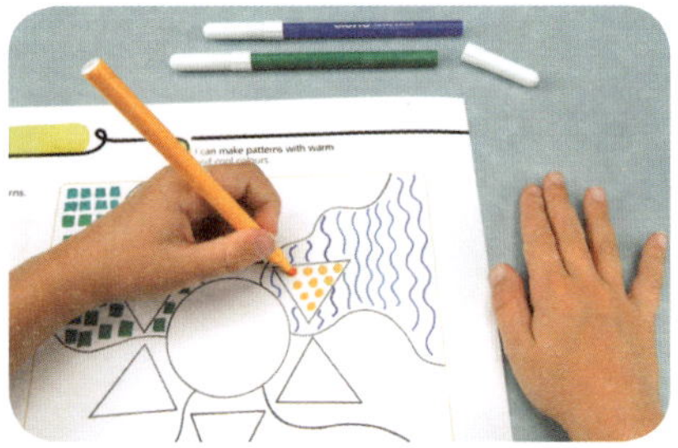

2. Make new cool colour patterns.

3. Make new warm colour patterns.

Finished?
Draw a pattern around a circle.

Sun mosaic

I can use small pieces of paper to make a mosaic.

Step 1

Put the warm and cool colours into groups.

Step 2

Glue the warm colours for the Sun.

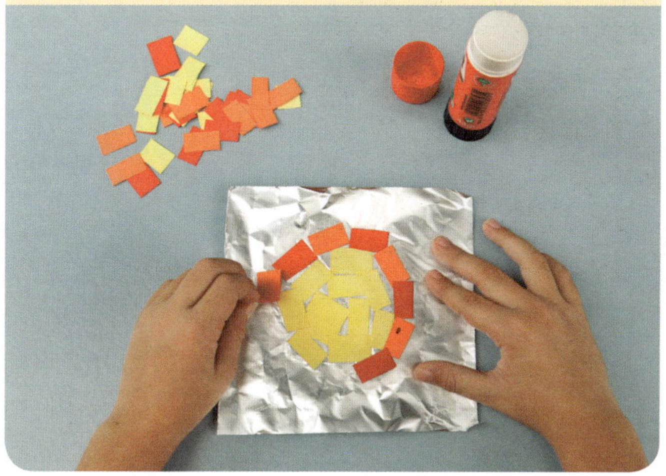

Step 3

Glue the cool colours around the Sun.

Finished? Make a mosaic of the moon.

REVIEW 3 Recycled Art

Teddy Bear, Leo Sewell. 1997

1 Read and match.

Artists can use different **materials** to make Art.

glass 1

fabric 2

metal 3

paper 4

plastic 5

wood 6

a 

d 

b 

e 

c 

f 

This artist uses **recycled materials**.

2

Which materials can you see in this recycled Art?

27 Activity 1 28 Activity 2

Make a recycled puppet

We can recycle materials to make Art.

Step 1

Cut and glue recycled paper.

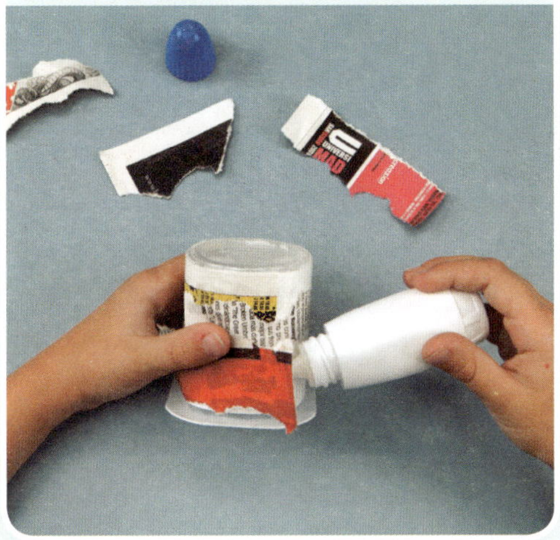

Step 2

Add a face.

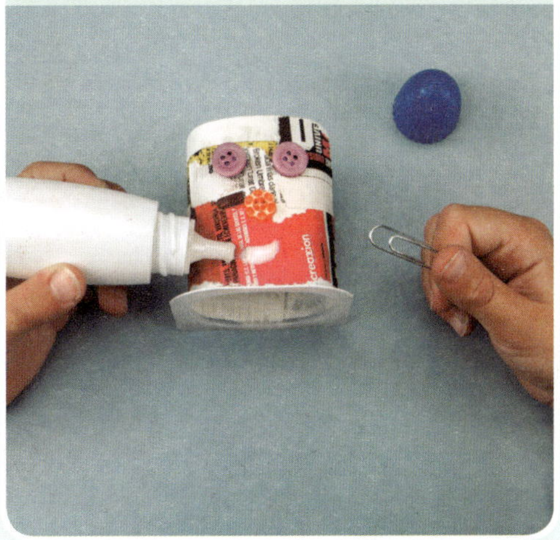

Step 3

Decorate.

Step 4

Add legs.

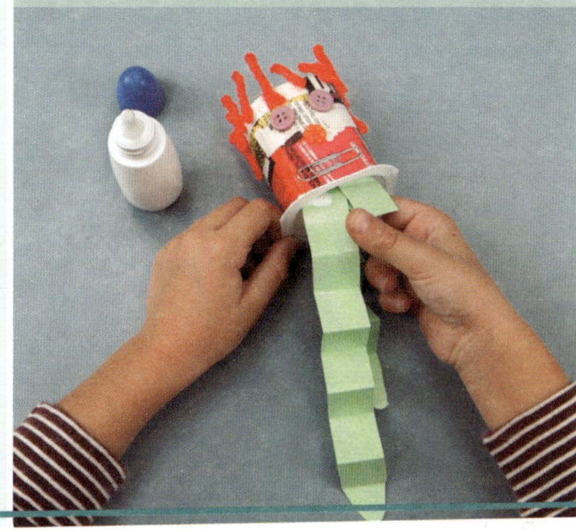

Finished? Add more recycled materials to your artwork.

My theatre

We can make a stage and tell a story with puppets.

Next step: Plan a story.

Step 5

Cut.

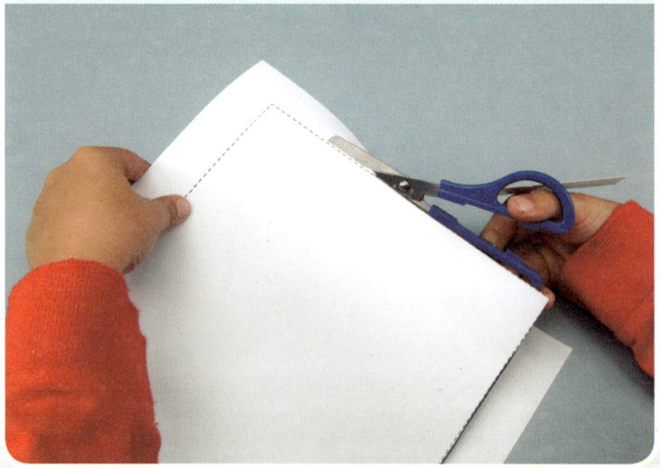

Step 6

Draw a scene and colour.

Step 7

Fold and glue.

Finished? Add objects to your stage.

Template page 73

Story time

Look at your artwork.

1 Read and tick.

My recycled art is made of:

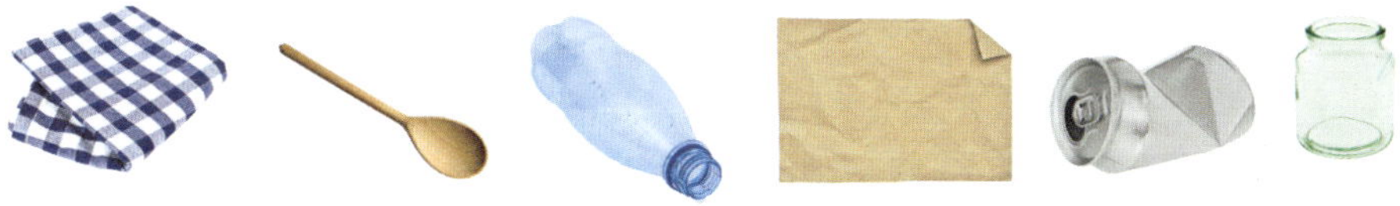

☐ ☐ ☐ ☐ ☐ ☐

2 Colour.

It's got warm colours and cool colours.

3 Draw.

I can see...

at the back

in the middle

at the front

Talk about your artwork.

Tell a story.

Halloween

My pumpkin is happy.
My pumpkin is sad.
My pumpkin is good.
My pumpkin is bad!

Step 1

Cut out and fold.

Step 2

Draw a face.

Step 3

Glue.

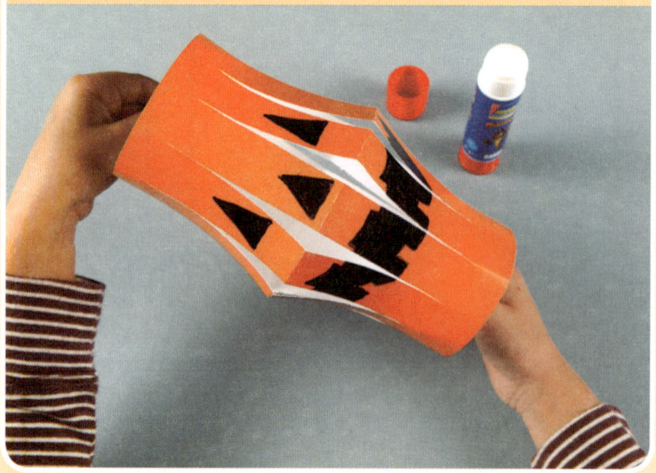

29 Chant
Halloween template **page 75**

Winter snowman

I've got eyes and a mouth.
I've got a nose, too.
I've got a hat and a scarf.
I'm looking at you.
I'm a snowman!

Step 1

Glue the white paper around the tube.

Step 2

Glue the hat and scarf.

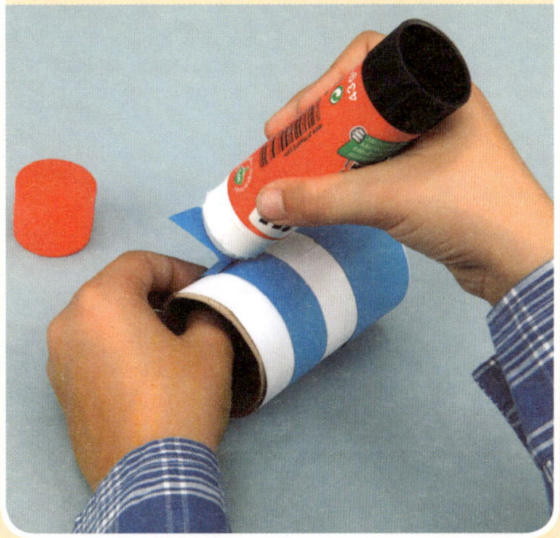

Step 3

Draw a face and buttons.

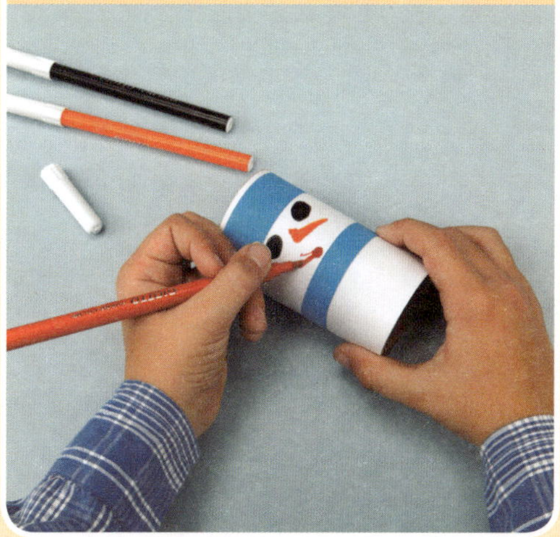

Step 4

Place in plasticine.

30 Chant

Christmas card

Christmas is here.
Let's decorate the tree.
We use lines, shapes and colours.
What patterns can you see?

Step 1

Draw and colour patterns in the shapes.

Step 2

Cut out.

Step 3

Glue the shapes in order.

31 Chant Christmas card template **page 77**

Peace Day

Hand with Flowers,
Pablo Picasso. 1958

Remember to share.
Remember to care.
Peace and love everywhere!

Step 1

Trace your hand.

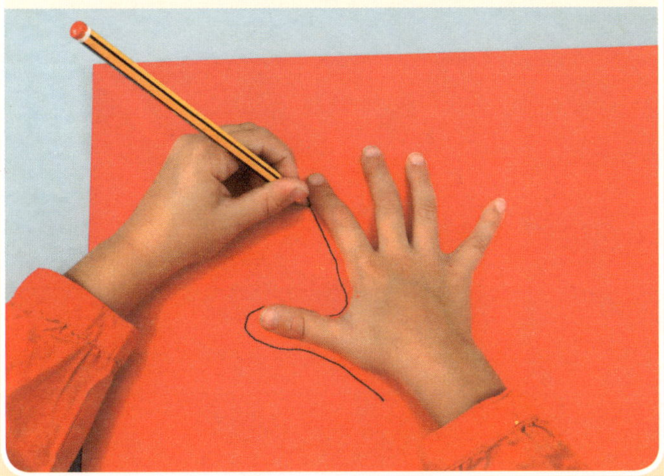

Step 2

Cut out.

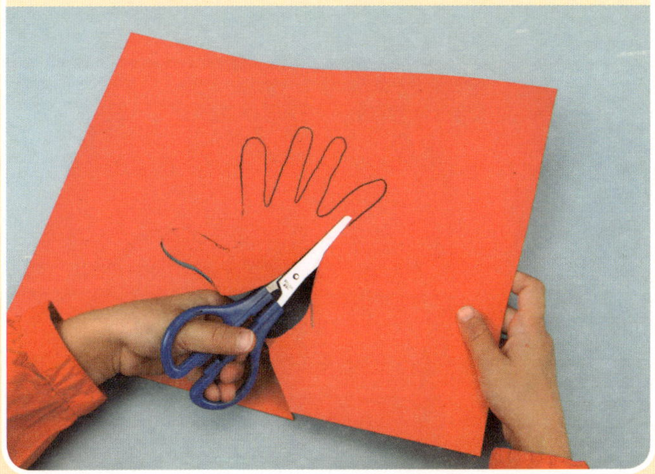

Step 3

Make a flower with friends.

32 Chant

Spring chick

It's got two black eyes.
It's got an orange beak.
It's got soft feathers.
It goes cheep, cheep, cheep!

Step 1

Decorate the egg.

Step 2

Colour the chick.

Step 3

Cut out and glue.

Step 4

Add a clip.

33 Chant
Spring chick template **page 79**

Summer fan

Hello summer.
Goodbye school.
Let's make fans
To keep us cool.

Step 1

Draw and colour a picture.

Step 2

Fold.

Step 3

Tape.

34 Chant

What can you see?

I can see...

There is / There are...

animals

plants

food

people

a landscape

a building

How do you feel?

I feel...

happy

sad

scared

What do you like best?

I like the...

It's got...

shapes

lines

patterns

colours

textures

forms

space

Paper

card

paper

tissue paper

Glue

glue stick

white glue

Mould

clay

plasticine

Cut and tear

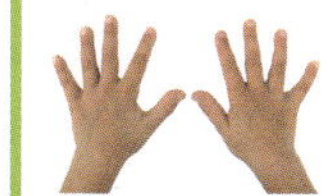
hands

scissors

Draw and colour

crayons

coloured pencils

felt tips

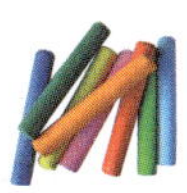
oil pastels

pencil

Paint

paintbrush

poster paint

water

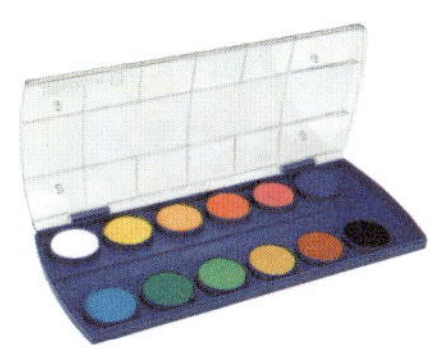
watercolours

Extra material

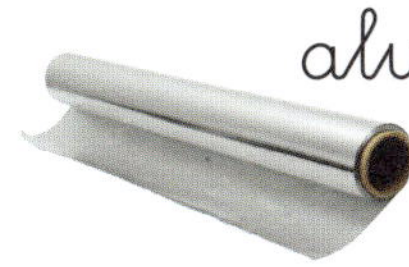
aluminium foil

box

clip

cord

glitter

paper roll

pencil sharpener

recycled materials

rubber

stickers

tape

Art techniques

Colour

Cut

Draw

Fold

Glue

Mould

Art techniques

Paint

Print

Rub

Tape

Tear

Tie

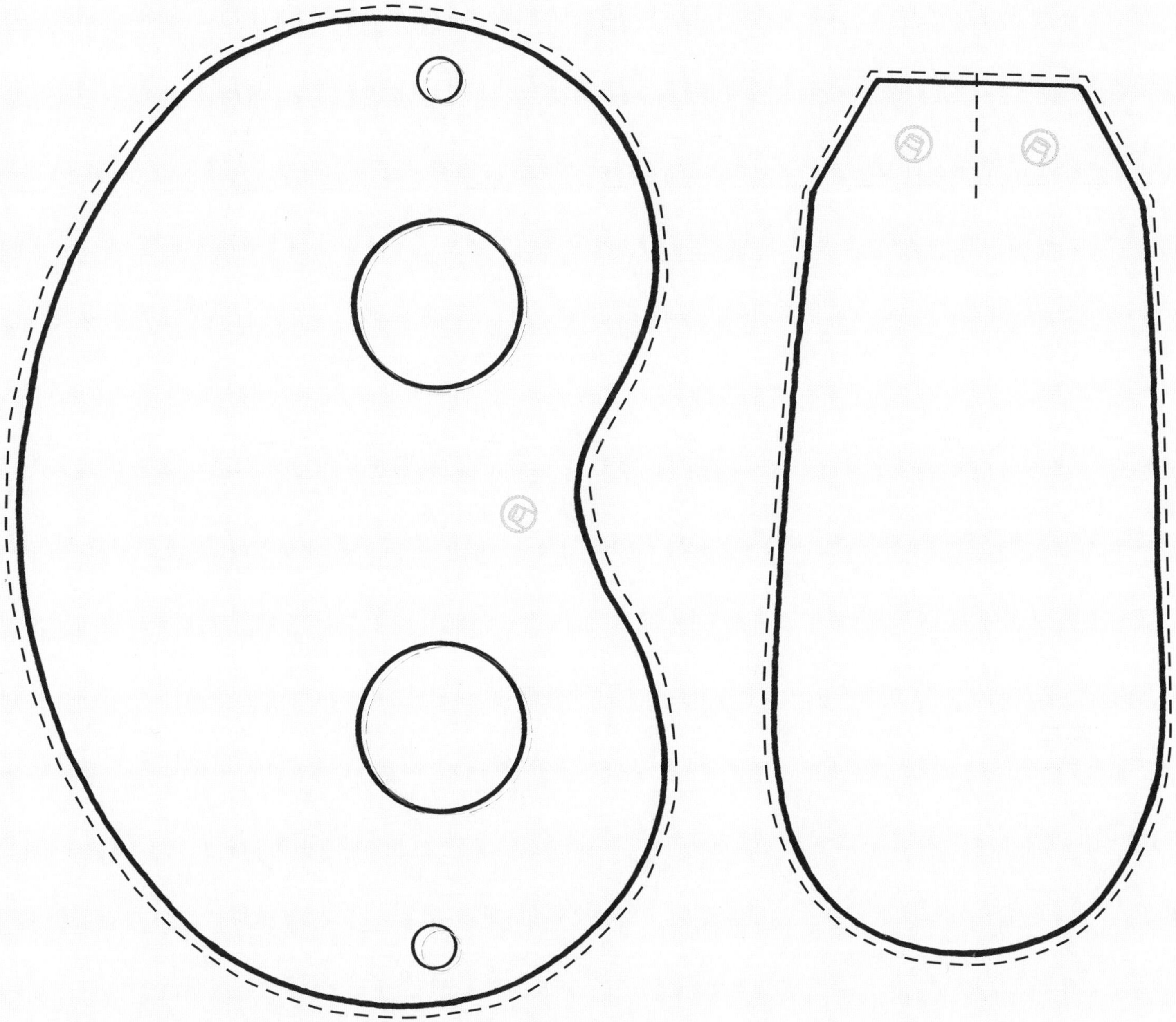

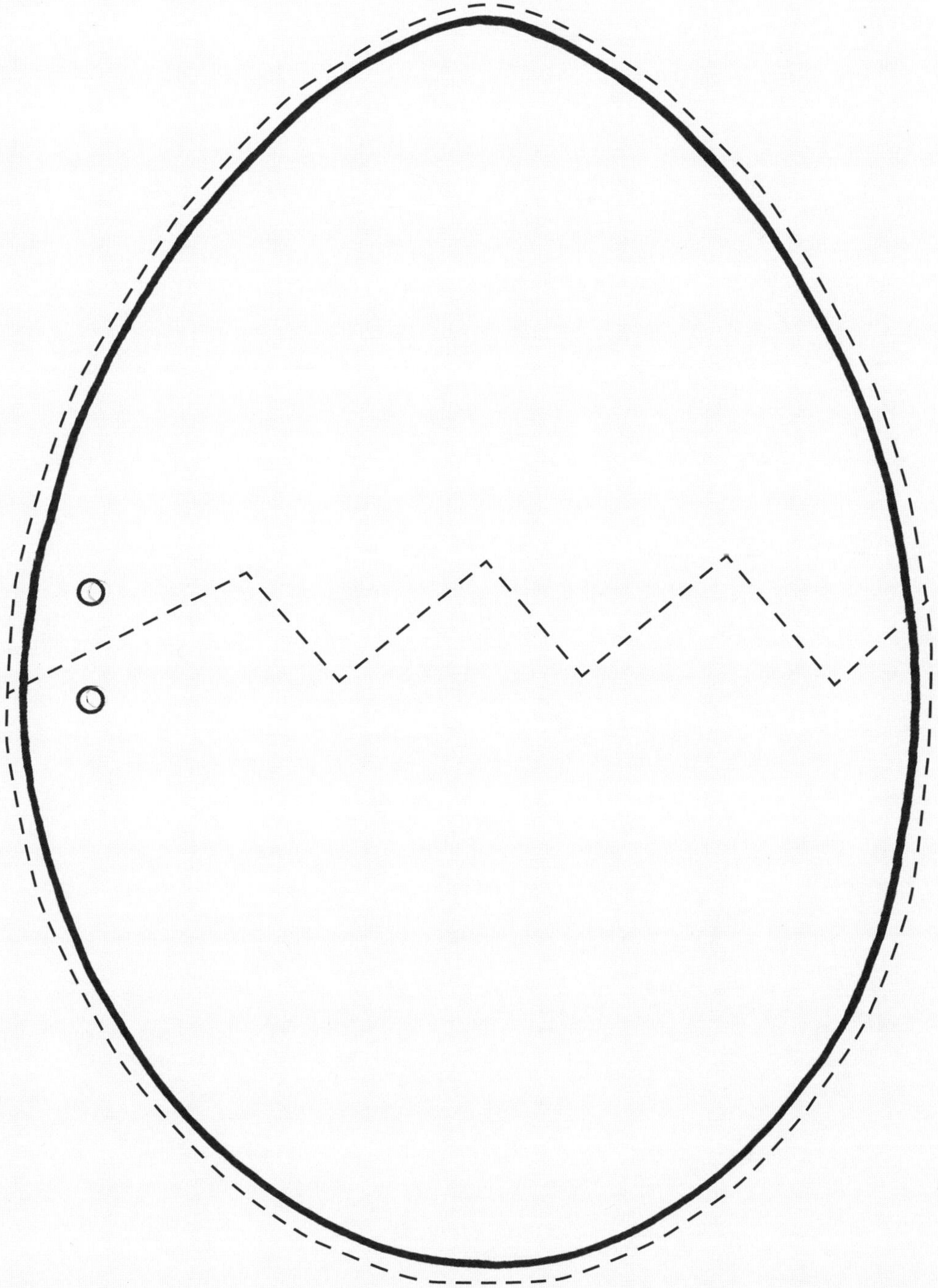